DISCARD

Koning, John W.

The manager looks
    at research
    scientists

$14.95

DATE			

THE MANAGER
LOOKS AT
RESEARCH
SCIENTISTS

THE MANAGER LOOKS AT RESEARCH SCIENTISTS

JOHN W. KONING, JR.

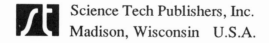
Science Tech Publishers, Inc.
Madison, Wisconsin   U.S.A.

John W. Koning, Jr.
4013 Naheda Trail
Madison, Wisconsin 53711

Library of Congress Cataloging-in-Publication Data

Koning, John W., Jr.
    The manager looks at research scientists / John W. Koning, Jr.
        p.   cm.
    Bibliography: p.
    Includes index.
    ISBN 0-910239-16-9
    1. Research--Management. 2. Scientists. I. Title
Q180.55.M3K55 1988
507'.2--dc19   88-2460
                                             CIP

Science Tech Publishers, Inc., Madison, Wisconsin U.S.A.

Printed in the United States of America

10 9 8 7 6 5 4 3 2 1

PREFACE

In 1974, I wrote an American Management Association Briefing entitled "A Scientist Looks at Research Management." It was based on a two-year study of a specific research organization, interviews with scientists, supervisors, and managers in other organizations, and a review of the literature on research management. Since then, I have had the opportunity--or better yet, the challenge--of putting into practice the ideas and concepts that were presented in that AMA briefing. Needless to say, things did not work out quite as suggested through the eyes of the scientist, but surprisingly better than I expected.

Since I moved from a supervisory position to a management position after writing the first briefing, I can now reread the first AMA briefing and look at it from a completely different perspective--in fact, really, from two. This new perspective leads me to some rather interesting reflections.

Thus, what I have done is to add reflections onto each section of the original writing. I have also added a major section of other aspects of management I learned the hard way. I call that subject "The Sticky Wickets".

I have deleted the original section on "A Personal Appraisal for the Supervisor". Not because the idea of direct feedback is flawed, but because in administering the appraisal, I found the employee is put in a no-win position.

I also realize that in my 1974 "Briefing" all the references were male-oriented. Since I reproduce the 1974 "Briefing" verbatim I haven't changed that--but it is important to note that my comments refer to both males and females, and I have tried to use each gender alternately from section to section.

John W. Koning, Jr.

About the Author

John W. Koning, Jr., is a Program Coordinator for the Engineering Professional Development Department, College of Engineering, University of Wisconsin-Madison. Prior to his recent appointment he was a Scientist, Project Leader for Packaging Research, and Assistant Director for Chemistry and Paper Research at the U.S. Forest Products Laboratory in Madison.

His responsibilities included administering the research programs in the areas of pulping, papermaking, wood chemistry, paper physics, packaging, and biotechnology. This included over 60 scientists and support people and a budget of over three million dollars.

He has written over 37 publications, is a guest lecturer, and has participated in a number of industrial seminars. He has presented papers at numerous conferences of the Technical Association of the Pulp and Paper Industry (TAPPI). In 1985 he was elected a Fellow of TAPPI. He also served on the Board of Directors of that organization (1985-1987).

In his seven years as a manager, his staff doubled their publication output, increased the number of publications in refereed journals, more than doubled the number of patents, and received numerous awards including the prestigious Wallenberg Prize. But of more importance, his staff solved or helped solve some real, significant problems.

A few examples are:

1. The development of the first usable performance standard for the shipping of commercial goods by common carrier. This has been adopted by ASTM D-10 and used by a number of companies with reported yearly savings in the thousands of dollars

2. The rapid acceleration of a new industry in the U.S. for the growing of *shiitake* mushrooms. This has resulted in new jobs and an economic boost for some rural areas. Research continues on the commercial production of these mushrooms on wood chips.

3. The isolation of the lignin-degrading enzyme. This research is being commercialized by at least one company. The potential for these enzymes in the pulp and paper industry, although big, may be insignificant when compared to their use as an agent for detoxifying wastewater and breaking down other toxic wastes such as dioxin, PCBs, and DDT. This latter discovery has the potential of saving billions of dollars for the taxpayer and industry.

4. The development of the first method to determine the biaxial strength of paper when loaded in the compression-compression mode. This fundamental research forms the base for improving the fundamental strength of paper and could lead to significant savings in the utilization of wood fiber.

5. The invention of a totally new form of a paper structural material, which was named "FPL Spaceboard". This material has great strength-to-weight ratio and has almost unlimited applications. Development continues on this breakthrough to produce it on a continuous basis.

ACKNOWLEDGMENTS

It is impossible to list all the people who have influenced this work, but I would like to acknowledge some who have made special contributions.

First is Herb Fleischer, Director of FPL (1967-1975), who appointed me chairman of the task group of scientists that made the 1974 AMA Briefing possible.

Second is Bob Youngs, Director of FPL (1975-1984), who gave me a chance to be a manager.

Third is John Erickson, Present Director of FPL, who reviewed this present work and made helpful suggestions.

I would also like to recognize the critical review by Hank Montrey, who was previously with Weyerhaeuser Co. and is now the Deputy Director of FPL, and Al Foulger, Assistant Director of the Northeast Forest and Range Experiment Station.

Special thanks go to Celeste Kirk for editing and to Jane Kohlman for typing and layout.

Finally, I dedicate this book to my wife Jane, who has been supportive throughout my career.

CONTENTS

"Nothing in the world can take the place of <u>persistence</u>. Talent will not; nothing is more common than unsuccessful men with talent. Education will not; the world is full of educated derelicts. <u>Persistence</u> and determination alone are omnipotent. The slogan 'press on' has solved, and always will solve, all problems."

(Calvin Coolidge)

THE MANAGER LOOKS AT RESEARCH SCIENTISTS

1

Defining the Ideal Environment

1974 "The Scientist Observes"

The ideal research environment is not easily defined, or it would have been before now. Indeed there is no single ideal definition that applies precisely to all situations; however, there are certain basic factors that are essential. Although not definitive, the following criteria encompass most of these factors:

--A scientist or group of scientists should be assigned a real, significant problem that (1) is directly related to a specific goal of the organization, and (2) allows the scientist to develop his discipline or specialty.

--Within a problem area, scientists should be allowed the independence to develop studies necessary to solve the problem.

--Scientists should be supervised by knowledgeable scientists and administrators who show continuing interest in the work, who attempt to fulfill the individual needs of the scientists, and who make a sincere effort to provide all the physical and technical support the scientists require.

--Completely open communication should exist throughout the organization.

--Scientists should be given generous recognition for work well done, and, conversely, should be constructively criticized when work is done poorly.

These are the essential components of an ideal research environment. The remainder of this briefing deals with each of these factors from the viewpoint of the scientist. As each statement is discussed, it should be considered in terms of both the supervisor and the scientist.

It should be pointed out that an ideal environment will not guarantee a smooth-running operation. Conflicts of opinion and personality clashes are inevitable, and no matter how nearly ideal the environment is, the unending need to deal with problems remains for supervisors and employees alike.

Unfortunately, there are no easy solutions to supervisory problems, primarily because supervising others is one of the most difficult tasks human beings are called upon to do. Even with all the reported research and studies underway, there always seems to be an exception to every rule. Perhaps the best that can be hoped for is to stimulate the reader into giving the whole subject more thought and to suggest some guidelines toward helping him solve specific problems.

After an environment approaching the ideal has been established, it still remains for employees to conduct themselves as professionals, performing tasks with the highest degree of efficiency, creativity, and candor, if quality work is to result. But supervisors should not seize upon this statement as a crutch, blaming ineffective employees for every project failure. The employee contribution is essential, but it is not the only important factor in the creative situation. The true key to ideal research conditions is the motivation provided by supervisors alert to opportunities for improving the environment and eager to communicate with individual employees. So the responsibilities of supervisor and organization must be emphasized.

Though it is true that the creative results have to come from the employee, establishing an environment that will provide for extended creative thought is the real goal, and this is primarily a responsibility of management.

1988 "The Manager Reflects"

Reflections:

My original definition of the ideal environment is still valid and as a manager I don't see a need to change it.

Another attempt to define or describe the creative environment was made by Blake in 1978 (1). He elaborated on some of the reasons management has for seeking to improve the creativity of the organization, and emphasized many of the same aspects of an ideal research environment as reported in the 1974 "Briefing".

The manager's problem is still how to put these factors into practice.

The previously assumed responsibilities of the scientists "to conduct themselves as professionals, performing tasks with the highest degree of efficiency, creativity, and candor" has not been observed to the degree expected. One of the most disappointing observations I made as a manager was the number of "scientists" who were more concerned with the number of hours they worked rather than doing their job. The effective manager has a major role in weeding out those pseudo-scientists.

2

Real Assignments Serve Real Needs

1974 "The Scientist Observes"

Today more than ever before, young graduates who are beginning their careers in research seek organizations where they can tackle real, meaningful problems. They are asking what they will be working on and how their work will contribute to the improvement of society and/or the environment. They are interested in the overall picture and their place in it.

The importance to the scientist of the type of work he does is shown by a survey conducted by the Federal Council for Science Technology (1). Out of 51 categories of questions, the item ranked most important in a sample of 1,025 scientists and engineers was "I should have an opportunity to work on creative, challenging projects." Moreover, an opinion poll conducted by *Industrial Research* indicated "nature of the work" as the number one job consideration (2). These surveys, along with the opinions of other interviewed scientists, clearly suggest that one critical factor in managing for creativity is helping scientists select and work on real, significant problems.

1988 "The Manager Reflects"

Reflections:

The matter of conducting research on real assignments to solve real needs is just as important today as it was perceived in 1974. My perceptions of how these assignments should be made have been strengthened for me through my change in perspective.

Selection of Real Problems

The questions now arise: How do we determine the status of a problem? How do we know whether it is real and significant? This is best done by looking first at the broad objectives of the organization. In industry, the broadest goal is to make a profit or to gain a specific position in the marketplace; in government, to perform a needed service for a large number of people in an area where others cannot supply the service. These goals can then be broken down into more specific objectives. Does a company need research to improve a product or class of products, to develop a whole new line of items, or to introduce a new process? Does an agency need data in an unexplored area? What problems are involved?

Reflections:

Scientists expect to be assigned significant problems when they take on a new job and it is up to management to see that this is done. I am convinced that it is the job of the manager and senior scientists, not new scientists, to select the problems that need research; however, new scientists should be involved in the process. This is because managers have a broader view of the organization's goals and, hopefully, some vision of the future. Senior scientists can also make significant contributions in this selection process. The concept of hiring a young new scientist and giving her carte blanche is a luxury few can afford. If that is the mode the scientist wants, let her find another meal ticket. This may sound tough but it is really the best for all concerned.

Surprisingly, there are some managers who feel that all that is important is to hire a good person and they will not only perform well, but will also know what the important problems are. Except for the hiring of a senior scientist, this approach is poor. The college graduate just cannot be expected to possess the background experience to properly select the most significant problems. This is not only a prerogative, but a major responsibility of management. The better approach is for management to determine what the real problems or problem areas are, provide the staff to solve those problems, and provide the support required so that the problems can be solved efficiently and effectively.

Testing Problem Status

This analysis should provide a long list of problems for the researcher; the next task is to establish whether they are real and significant. Each problem must be tested rationally in terms of an organization's overall goals and the specific goals of its operating level. To make this test, the following questions should be answered as honestly as possible:

> --Will solution of this problem really help the organization accomplish its goals?
> --How important is it to the organization? To society?
> --Is anyone else doing it?
> --Will someone else do it?

--What is the probability of success?
--How much time will be required?
--If a solution is found, what will be the adoption rate?
--Will facilities and personnel be available and well used?
--Will solution of the problem result in a significant contribution to knowledge?
--How urgent is the problem?
--Who else will benefit?
--What are the alternatives?
--Will the benefits justify the costs of solution?

By answering these questions, or whatever others are pertinent in a specific situation, both management and scientists can arrive at a rational priority rating for selecting problems. This will help immensely to eliminate someone's pet project, confused staff direction, and fragmentation of effort.

Reflections:

The list of questions for testing problem status is still valid. These questions must be answered honestly.

Unfortunately, I find that some managers have difficulty with the "honestly" part. They don't lie; rather they throw out the list of questions, and write a new list, develop a complicated matrix approach (and bury everyone in activity), or "wing it".

From a management perspective, another question should be included, "What are the economic and political aspects?" I use 'political' in the broadest sense. One can invent the most sophisticated solution to a problem but still not have accomplished much. To accomplish something, it has to be not only technically acceptable but also be economically and politically acceptable. As we move from technical to economic to political, the logic patterns change; this can lead to great frustration for the scientist. A competent manager understands these differences in logic and will make adjustments during the technical developments so that the project has a chance of succeeding economically and politically. Once you recognize the importance of the three aspects of acceptance--technical, economical, and political--of a solution to be considered an accomplishment, the more quickly the senior scientists and managers will be able to do a good job of problem selection.

Unfortunately, many scientists have little feel for the economic or political aspects of a technical solution; too many supervisors and managers suffer from the same limited view. The reality of life, however, is that the person or organization that provides the funds for research has a responsibility to maximize the return on that investment and meet other objectives that may be purely political.

Working Together

In the process of choosing the research problems, it is important for the supervisor to work with scientists because their involvement in the selection of problems creates a strong motivation for enthusiasm and creativity. Also, the new graduate should not be overlooked in the selection process, for he can make a considerable contribution in rating the importance of a problem as a result of his more recent academic involvement.

The Career Service Board for Science puts it this way: "More than any other incentive or form of recognition, the opportunity for the scientist to have a voice in the conduct or kind of research in which he is involved is of primary importance to his professional status and feeling of involvement" (3).

In many organizations, decisions as to what projects are worthwhile are made by people completely removed from the immediate research environment. This is an unfortunate fact of life; one can only hope that these organizations will delegate more responsibility and authority to the lowest levels possible and thus involve more of their employees in the decision-making process.

Reflections:

In selecting problems, it is important for management to work with the scientific staff. This can be accomplished by group meetings that encourage the scientists' input to define the problem, but the final selection and setting of priorities is a necessary function of senior scientists and management. It has been observed that management is reluctant to do this job, particularly in setting priorities. "Why" is not completely clear. Part of this reluctance is genuine disagreement between managers. Part is the feeling that if Project A is given top priority, the people working on Project B or C are not as important. Hogwash!--it is, but real in the minds of some people. This problem of status and its importance was also observed and discussed by Allen in 1979 (4).

The important fact is that all activity has a relative priority and in no way is this priority of activity to be applied to the individual employee's personal worth. It is this conflict, or confusion, that leads to the problem when one sets priorities on activities and it is interpreted as setting priorities on people's worth. And yet, these two get mixed up to the point where they lead to a lot of personnel problems. But even at the risk of these problems, management must set priorities.

Working together also invokes the idea of team research. In a conversation with one of my supervisors, he brought up the subject of team research and concentration of resources and how much further we would be if we had done this a few years ago. This started me thinking, admittedly a bit defensively, since I had obviously chosen not to do this. I reflected on other research organizations around the world, especially a couple that had unsuccessfully tried putting teams on specific, difficult problems. I realized that apparently one of the major reasons our staff had been successful was that we did not generally embrace this approach; rather, we went in the opposite direction and encouraged great diversity.

Rather than create teams, I had challenged each scientist to make his mark, and the response was tremendous, as indicated by each of their accomplishments. One of the best things I did as a manager was to try to have each scientist have at least two very difficult, but important, problems to solve. I wish I could write here that I was smart enough to have planned this course of diversity but the fact is that I backed into it. This was because top management gave no clear goals, scientists were rated on individual accomplishments, our clients said they wanted basic research but really wanted applied research, we had a decreasing budget, there were no incentives for team research, and two in-house attempts at team research had been near disasters.

Given the requirement for immediate accomplishments, it was not wise to support two or three big research problems when budgets are a yearly affair. Rather, encouraging 25 scientists to creatively tackle approximately 50 real, significant and difficult problems, I played the odds that we might hit on at least one or two a year and then develop these breakthroughs. This seems to have worked.

I was also motivated by the quote by J. Roethke:

"What we need are more people who specialize in the impossible."

The staff responded in exciting ways except for a few who were not creative, were over-the-hill, or were "pseudo-scientists". These either retired or were encouraged to seek other careers where their talents could be better used. I might add that those who sought other careers have all done well, and certainly better than if they had stayed in the research environment. Unfortunately, I also lost a couple of top scientists who voluntarily chose retirement.

My ultimate view of teamwork is that its appropriate place is after the initial breakthrough is accomplished, when the creative idea needs development. Just be sure there are rewards in your organization for teamwork.

Development of Individual Disciplines

Discipline has a number of definitions, both broad and narrow. Here the term means the particular skill or specialty acquired through the academic training or experience that the scientist brings to the job. It is imperative that he be encouraged to keep his specialty finely honed by being allowed to use his skills. An obvious reason is that these skills are essential to a supervisor for solving the problems facing the organization. Another reason, not so obvious but just as important, is that if the scientist loses his marketable skills, through disuse, misuse, or very narrow application, he quickly loses motivation for meaningful work. This loss does not mean he will quit producing; on the contrary, in terms of quantity it may have a temporary quickening effect. However, his solutions to problems will lack true creativity; he will weigh ideas not in terms of solving the problem but in terms of how they will suit his supervisor.

Obviously from time to time in every organization scientists are asked to work on an insignificant job. This is particularly true for scientists who have administrative responsibilities and for those who work in small organizations where service groups are small or nonexistent. It should be remembered that every job carries with it many petty but necessary tasks. However, it should also be remembered that if such insignificant assignments become the pattern or the primary way the scientist uses his time, his creativity will eventually be turned off, and he will very quickly begin to devote his creative energy to something other than the organization's goals.

Thus developing disciplines is important and demands a conscientious effort by supervisor and employee alike. What can be done?

Reflections:

From a manager's point of view, development of individual disciplines is important but it is difficult to accomplish. Elaborate training plans are used by some organizations but the paperwork tends to discourage its effective use. More emphasis is placed on properly filled out forms than good development programs.

Another facet of the problem is the perception scientists have of themselves. As a new supervisor, one may find it difficult to do effective career planning with an older scientist, especially if the previous supervisors did little to help this scientist's career. Even worse is when one inherits "pseudo-scientists" whom the previous supervisors never leveled with. These are the real-life situations and probably explain why some companies conduct wholesale layoffs that seem capricious. It is one way of starting fresh with new employees and supervisors to try to get the system to function creatively again.

Thus, realistic career counseling is essential to achieving a good research climate. How do you tell the good scientists that they are limited as supervisors because of their lack of ability to work with other people? Or, do you tell them at all?

This is particularly difficult if you work for an organization that requires movement into a supervisory position for promotion. Fortunately there are a number of organizations that have dual ladder arrangements where a scientist can move up in the organization without being a supervisor. My experience though has indicated that you go farther in an organization on the management ladder.

One approach is to set up a series of criteria that will be used to judge their advancement. This will include not only what you want to accomplish in the work, but also other activities, to let the scientists try to develop their interpersonal skills. Frankly, this sounds easy, but it isn't. And even with a small number of scientists, it is very time-consuming.

This same situation holds true for changing or broadening a scientist's skills in science. It can be done through course work, seminars, sabbaticals, and working with other scientists, but it is a time-consuming task to coordinate this with the research that needs to be accomplished. A major part of the problem is motivating supervisors to invest the time in their scientists development.   Generally, the organization does not reward this activity except with lip service.

In fact, career development is one of the most "talked-about and nothing-done-about" areas in management. Everyone is for it, but little happens. If employees push it, their loyalty is questioned as they are suspected of having too much free time to think. But even more frustrating is when a manager decides that career development is in the best interest of the company and employee, and decides to do something about it. Immediately, one finds that although there is a lot of literature on career development, much of it is difficult to apply.

For example, one of the first hurdles is that good career planning actually involves life planning and with privacy laws the process has to be purely voluntary on the part of the employee. Second, there is a major question of who should handle career or life planning--i.e., personnel, immediate supervisor, second-level manager, outside counselor. There are real pros and cons for each of these positions handling the planning. I feel that the second-level manager is the appropriate person.

Also confounding this area is the fact that so many employees have a spouse who works and it is impossible to do life planning without the spouse's involvement.   Life planning is a must and it is to management's advantage to encourage it.   However, having tried to implement career planning, I could not find a really good workbook; one has recently been developed by the Technical Association of the Pulp and Paper Industry (TAPPI) in Atlanta, Georgia. However, in essence, career or life planning still remains the primary responsibility of the individual.

Use Special Skills Effectively.

The concept of developing a specialty or skill, as well as personal goals, should be discussed with each scientist. It stands to reason that he was hired because of his expertise in a particular area, and an attempt should be made to apply that special knowledge to pertinent projects. Such arrangements should be made for all his major assignments. This is obvious and logical, but more often than not, management, after making such arrangements at the outset, subsequently tends to forget, and assigns him to projects outside the scope of his interests.

Granted, short-term assignments outside a scientist's discipline or on its fringes may sometimes be necessary, even desirable, since they help to broaden one's perspective. But such practices should be watched so that they do not get out of hand. Frequent assignments outside the scientist's discipline are a particularly easy habit for the supervisor to fall into when task-force approaches to problem-solving are used.

Reflections:

I still agree with my earlier thoughts on this use of talent, but I find that it takes constant management vigilance not to slip the scientist into an area that needs work but does not make use of her specific skills.

Unfortunately, further training is one of the first activities to go when the budget is tight. Realistically that is proper, but it can only be a solution for the short term. Things change, and it is important that your staff is up to date. One inexpensive opportunity is on-the-job training and another is short courses; a good manager will help uncover other possibilities. We must be particularly wary of the supervisor who talks a good game of employee development but never can let any of her staff participate in training or, worse yet, makes a mockery of it by allowing an employee to attend a one-day course every other year. It sounds ridiculous, but I can cite even worse examples.

Continue Building Skills

The scientist should be allowed time to do active research strictly in his discipline no matter what the nature of his other assignments. Discipline-oriented research may not occupy the greater part of the scientist's time, but some time is essential. In this respect a strict time schedule is not advocated. Primarily the need is for the supervisor to convey his genuine concern that the scientist schedule his time to allow for research in his discipline. This attitude will go a long way in building a scientist's confidence in his supervisor because it engenders mutual trust.

If, in frank discussions, the scientist shows a desire to change his discipline--for example, from one branch of chemistry to another--then his supervisor should try to assign him a problem in which he can explore the desired shift. The problem, however, must be a real one and one that will help the project or organization meet its goals. If a change is impossible, the supervisor should explain the situation to the scientist as soon as possible and give the real reasons why.

Perhaps a short-term problem in a new field can be assigned. If work on this problem indicates that a shift will be beneficial to the organization and to him, and a transfer becomes possible from the organization's standpoint, specific training should be pursued in the new discipline.

The scientist's strengths and weaknesses should be discussed with him. He needs to know where he stands with his supervisor and top management. A yearly comment such as, "Keep up the good work and some day you'll get promoted", though better than nothing, is far from sufficient.

The supervisor should encourage the scientist to select, join, and become actively involved in professional societies that will keep him abreast of advances in technology. In addition to technical conferences, these societies provide him with valuable contacts with others in the field who can help solve future problems. There is a lot of truth in the statement that the most valuable aspect of a technical conference is the contact between scientists in related fields rather than the papers presented. The scientist should also continue his education through formal and informal courses, travel, and contact with other scientists who are working on similar problems.

In addition to choosing real problems and developing the scientist's discipline, it is important to allow him the independence within a problem area to develop studies necessary to solve the problem. This aspect of the ideal environment for creative research is discussed in the next section.

Reflections:

Building on skills is still an important activity.

One of my major jobs as a manager was trying to get increased funding for travel, especially foreign, and for participation in professional organizations. I have purposefully coupled these two subjects because the major hindrance to participating in professional organizations is travel funds. Frankly it irritated me constantly to have to continuously fight for travel funds. Thirty years ago, one may have been able to argue that scientists didn't need to travel, particularly to foreign countries, but that day is long gone, if it really existed at all. It is essential for scientists to get involved and find out what is going on. We are all now part of a global society. The same rationale goes for active participation in professional organizations. Scientists have to get involved if they want to keep abreast and make things happen.   By active participation, I mean joining committees of interest and *Volunteering* for task group and subcommittee assignments.   This is where the leading edge action is going to happen and this is how real networks are formed; they will serve a scientist the rest of her career.

I feel so strongly about travel that I would suggest that the next time an opening occurs in your unit, the manager should see if she can get the salary money released so she can properly support existing scientists. Hiring another person will just dilute the support budget.

If you still aren't convinced, ask yourself, "How did the Japanese move so fast after the war?"   Simply, 1) dedication to quality, 2) awareness of what's going on in the world, helped greatly by extensive foreign travel, and 3) hard work. We are in trouble in the U.S. auto industry; could yours be next?

As a manager, I see one small problem to be aware of: that of a scientist getting "carried away" and spending all his time on society activities at the expense of the primary research assignments. The important thing is proper balance and time allocation. The judicious use of travel funds can help solve this problem. However, it is better to err on too much involvement in society activities than not enough.

3

Free Range for the Creative Mind

1974 "The Scientist Observes"

"Freedom for the researcher to carry out his work as he sees fit is generally regarded as a primary environmental variable and is at the core of most study recommendations" (1). If complete details of the method and cost by which the scientist is to approach the problem or to solve it are required or imposed upon him prior to starting, creativity will be stifled. Despite this emphasis on creativity, it should be clearly understood that the real life of a scientist has only moments of pure creative thought and days of hard, tedious, even frustrating work. Thus continuing interest and encouragement by the supervisor--rather than dogmatic and rigid rules--are especially vital.

1988 "The Manager Reflects"

Reflections:

Thus, if you want creative solutions to real, significant problems then give each scientist a challenge of at least two difficult problems, get out of their way, and give them support. If they are true scientists, you won't be disappointed; if they are incapable, it will become apparent.

A Voice in Procurement

If equipment or supplies are arbitrarily restricted, even for approved studies, the administration is in effect saying, "Be

19

creative, but do it without the risk of any expenditures on tangible items." This statement may sound ridiculous, but it happens every day. Balderston states, "The working scientist knows the frustration that comes from trying to justify an expensive piece of research equipment to a nontechnical man who seeks to determine for it a return on investment or a utilization factor. He knows the cost in lost enthusiasm and in unrecoverable time to those endless delays that are caused by the 'system'. Perhaps he has felt, at times, that the accountants are really running the laboratory" (2).

Often the administrator's position seems to be that if he lets his staff have freedom to buy equipment and supplies, the organization will be bankrupt overnight. This attitude evokes some unfortunate assumptions by the scientist. He may believe that, although he is classified as a professional, the administration does not really trust his judgment. Or it assumes that, if a few scientists have questionable judgment, no chances should be taken by granting purchasing freedom to any of them.

This attitude also suggests to the scientist that the supervisor is not completely sure that he has selected a real problem. For if he were, he would be convinced that solution of the problem is very important to the organization and worth any reasonable cost.

Excessive caution in granting scientists authority for expenditures also indicates the supervisor's lack of understanding of true creative research. He simply cannot appreciate the fact that with any real breakthrough go many setbacks and failures, and there can be no guarantee that equipment purchases will result in success.

Even in an organization where supervisors do have working budgets, purchasing procedures can still restrict a scientist's creativity. If administrative procedures require him to obtain one or more approvals for every requisition, he has no real independence. Granted, new employees should have a ceiling on spending, but they should not be insulted by having to get approvals for each small requisition. A petty cash fund should be available to take care of minor expenditures. As the scientist demonstrates his ability to solve problems and to handle funds responsibly, his ceiling should be raised. Progressively providing more freedom to purchase materials and services is a strong incentive to the scientist to produce, because it indicates management's support and contributes to his feeling of worth.

Another often overlooked aspect of the purchasing responsibility is the positive reaction of the staff when a piece of equipment is acquired that really does improve the organization's efficiency. The supervisor should let the scientist know how he feels about the purchase, especially if management did not originally support its acquisition. It doesn't hurt for management to admit that the scientist was right about a given investment in equipment.

Carte blanche acquisition of facilities and equipment is not advocated. In fact, maximum use should be made of existing facilities at other laboratories, especially if the desired equipment has a high initial or operating cost and the needs are for one-time or short-time use. It is better to pay the fee and rent time on the equipment for long-range savings, particularly when the work is truly creative and thus has a high risk of failure.

This reasoning is also sound in the area of technical support. One should not hire a full-time specialist unless there is sufficient justification. Consideration should be given first to the part-time services of a consultant, university professor, or specialist whose time and salary can be shared with other organizations. Fees are often high but, considering the higher cost of a full-time person to handle the specialized material, it may be a savings to the organization in the long run.

Reflections:

One of the major reasons supervisors have trouble motivating their scientists is their inability to deal with the devastating negative effect purchasing has on scientists' creativity and organizational momentum. I studied this area for nine months and found that the organization had purposely set up an accountability system that was outside the normal chain of command, thus effectively neutralizing or at least slowing down management's ability to move effectively. The reasons were numerous, and unfortunately real (in the U.S. government and I'm sure also in industry); we have to comply with this or that regulation or law. Never mind that all the supposed savings by complying with these rules and laws were lost many times over by long delays in project completions, lost enthusiasm, and major cost overruns to fix, rebuild, or modify the work or equipment procured by someone less knowledgeable than the scientist who was to use it.

The only solution to this problem is to return purchasing to its proper role: It exists to facilitate the purchasing deemed necessary by management and the scientist.

Another way that will help is to set up individual budgets for each scientist with the amount dependent on their demonstrated ability to properly manage the funds.

Freedom to Organize Time

In many creative endeavors, management's insistence on strict adherence to rigid working hours is questionable. Except in organizations with enlightened leadership, it seems that some managers believe that creativity can be turned on at 8 or 9 AM and off at 4 or 5 PM. It doesn't work that way. A better approach is described by Balderston: "We sought an atmosphere of academic freedom for the senior scientific staff, while retaining stricter control on working hours and working conditions for the administrative staff and the laboratory technicians" (3).

As a scientist demonstrates his responsibility, he is given a new area of involvement and possibly a title. Why not really make the recognition meaningful by letting him have freedom to set his own hours? This concept of open hours should also apply to the younger, responsible scientists and senior technicians; it should be a reward for good work, not age.

It is necessary to trust the scientist's judgment about his working hours. It just doesn't make sense to treat a highly paid professional as an hourly employee.

A responsible scientist will give many more hours than the 30 to 40 required. He was hired to solve problems creatively, not to make a timesheet look neat and complete. If he is untrustworthy, the quality of his work will quickly reflect it.

The division of a scientist's time between his "bench" and his office is another area in which full independence should be granted. Autocratic dictums that scientists are to be at their desks thinking and writing, and technicians are to do the bench work indicates a lack of understanding of the process of creative endeavor. Scientists must "get their hands dirty on occasion."

The more complex calculations are within the scientist's province if he wants them to be, and his freedom to work on his own data is important. Restriction of this freedom is increasing with increased use of automation. Some centralization is necessary in our increasingly complex world, but the concept of centralized computing of all data is questionable. It introduces the risk of missing important findings and often adds delays that snuff out the scientist's enthusiasm. On the other hand, all routine calculations should be done by a technician and full use of computing services for this type of work is essential.

Remember that the job of the supervisor is to create the proper environment--but that creativity cannot be forced. The challenge of the problem, the opportunity to solve it, and the scientist's inherent creative urge are the determining factors.

Reflections:

To really have an ideal research environment, it is important that the scientists be able to set their own hours. This assumes that the employee is a true professional and is conducting genuine research. Unfortunately, this is not always the case; in fact, it seems that the ones who consider themselves great scientists are the very ones who shave the work hours when given a chance. What surprises me is that there are more than a few employees who want to be considered top scientists but refuse to earn it through genuine accomplishments.

Creative Supervision

Although an ideal research environment is made up of many factors, the lack of a good immediate supervisor will negate the whole effort. He may be responsible for several kinds of scientists; besides the truly creative scientists there are the engineers and other scientists who are essential in bringing others' thoughts to fruition. They have the essential ability to complete the tedious work, to bounce back after the frustrating failures to try again. All these people are essential, and it is the supervisor's tremendous job to motivate, utilize, and properly supervise them so that the best interests of the organization and the individuals are served.

As demanding as this task is, it is not impossible. People need the approval of other people, scientists no less than others. The acquisition of things outwardly suggesting success--the prestigious title, the private parking space, and, to some extent, salary--is sought after less for their value than for the recognition they bring to the owner. Hinrichs has already noted this aspect (4) and, while he discusses it in an industrial setting, it is equally true in academic or government situations. Only the symbols change; the motivation remains the same.

For the scientist, his work is what he wishes to be recognized for and known by. His measure of success is the extent to which its value is realized and applauded by his peers. His motivation, over the long haul, is the extent to which his work is rewarded and supported by his immediate supervisor and, to a lesser degree, by top management.

Reflections:

As a scientist, I felt that the immediate supervisor was critical to providing an ideal environment; I still do. But the difficulty of being a good supervisor is greater than I originally assumed.

When management is selecting a new supervisor, the following list of skills should be considered, and if any strong or even moderate deficiencies in these items appears, another candidate should be selected.

Flexibility	(Critical)
Interpersonal skills	(Critical)
Communication skills	(Critical)
Vision	(Critical)
Enthusiasm	(Critical)
Persistence	(Critical)
Productivity	(Critical)
Company interests	(Important)
Outside contacts	(Important)
Organization	(Important)
Teamwork	(Important)
Inside contacts	(Important)
Technical expertise	(Desirable)
Paperwork skills	(Necessary)

It is important to note the low position "technical" has on the list. Drucker (1974) went so far as to suggest that "to manage innovation, a manager need not be a technologist" (5). I don't agree with Drucker that it is not necessary, but it isn't as important as some scientists think it is. A good supervisor, with effort, can learn the essential technical aspects.

Also, since top scientists are often being considered for supervisory positions, they will have already demonstrated their technical competence. Future success as a supervisor will not be determined primarily by the continued technical competence of the supervisor--although with the current demise of middle managers I strongly recommend that any supervisor keep current in at least one area of expertise.

Another aspect of this problem is how the company management measures and rewards good supervision. This is one of the root causes of disenchanted supervisors. When rewards are not forthcoming, there is little real incentive to be an outstanding supervisor. We, as managers, have to reward the good supervisors.

Being interested in research management, I have long wondered why so many excellent scientists make such poor supervisors. On the basis of personal observations, there seems to be a number of major problems.

--Lack of flexibility. First, and I think foremost, is that a scientist has greater difficulty dealing with degrees of correctness rather than right or wrong. A scientist's professional life is spent dealing with facts, dealing with things, and observing specific occurrences. When the observation is not a proven fact, much time is spent determining the reliability of the observations; obviously a major emphasis is on the importance of specificity.

Now, take that same scientist and make her a supervisor. The first major shock is that she has to deal with other humans, and right and wrong take on new dimensions. The existence of personnel rules and regulations, budget guidelines, travel restrictions, etc., all imply that it's business as usual, follow every rule, that's right, that's wrong. But humans--and especially creative scientists--are not things and they do not conform passively to rules and regulations. All of a sudden, the supervisor has to face the reality that everything does not have a right or wrong answer. Many just can't live with this dichotomy. And to make matters worse, management not only expects this simultaneous dichotomy of thinking, but often doesn't recognize the conflict this sets up in the scientist-turned-supervisor's mind.

The worst situation is one in which management insists that the person both be a good supervisor and continue to be an excellent scientist. All this does is reinforce the conflict. Occasionally a person can handle both, but unfortunately it is uncommon. Generally some middle manager covers for the supervisor's deficiency but, with fewer middle manager positions in the flatter organization structures, this problem will become greater.

--Lack of interpersonal skills. Much of management deals with people and personnel problems; most scientists work with things or data. There is a big difference.

--Lack of communications skills. Many scientists and engineers avoid English or speech-type courses; they prefer the "bench". Managers need to communicate in all modes. Actually scientists and engineers need to also but it is difficult to convince them until it negatively affects their careers.   Thus, as a scientist-turned-supervisor quickly finds out, communication is critical.

--Lack of vision. The scientist has a good grasp of his or her area but many times does not have the ability to look at other areas and integrate this information in terms of the future.

--Lack of management continuity. Continued attempts by top management to apply the latest management fad is difficult enough for the management-minded supervisor, especially when the fad receives top management's word of support but not personal acceptance. The same thing leaves the scientist-turned-supervisor confused and frustrated.

Furthermore, creative supervision demands an inordinate amount of time.

This list could be expanded but I'll have more to say on this later. In fact, the section on "The Sticky Wickets" deals with many of these problems that make it difficult for a scientist to be a good supervisor.

After eight years as a supervisor and then as a manager, I can reflect on how green the grass is on the management side of the fence. To be honest, it is greener on the scientists' side--unless you really prefer working on personnel problems, paperwork, meeting agendas, budgets, etc., rather than solving real, significant problems. (If you're a real scientist, I doubt that you will prefer this, in spite of the money.)

Interest Sparks Response

How do you turn off a scientist? Assign him a task without any explanation for the assignment; then accept his report on the completed work and tell him you are too busy to discuss it. On the surface this episode seems harmless and petty, but it is not. The scientist interprets this seemingly disinterested attitude as, "What you have been doing is all right, I guess, but I'm really not too interested since the problem I assigned you is of questionable significance."

Admittedly there are times when a manager is genuinely busy, and the scientist should understand this. The manager may have problems with his own research, inadequate understanding of the research method being used, personal problems, or even problems with his own supervisor. However, the scientist doesn't know these reasons, and shouldn't be expected to know them. He takes this apparent disinterest as a discouraging indication that his work is not important and that the supervisor is not concerned about his development.

You may believe that this complaint cannot be a true one, or it would be heard more often from scientists. Actually, in most management situations, no scientist is likely to confront a supervisor with it. When he is seriously considering leaving his job, he may bring it up, but by then their relationship will have deteriorated so far that discussion is pointless.

An effective supervisor finds the time to discuss his scientist's work with him. The very act of making time for this important task will go a long way toward developing and maintaining the worker's enthusiasm. An effective supervisor gets out of his office and finds out what's going on; he talks to his people informally and frequently. If he depends on formal reports to evaluate work, he is overlooking an excellent communications device to encourage creativity: An honest show of interest in the work by observing and discussing it on the spot.

Reflections:

I have observed that one of the most powerful motivating tools a supervisor has is genuine interest in her scientists' research and personal development.

As a scientist, I could never understand why the supervisor, and especially the manager, didn't take much interest in the active research. I still don't. I must admit it isn't easy and some scientists are not easy to interact with, but that is part of the job. The bigger problem is the time demands placed on the supervisor and manager to attend meetings, to travel, and to complete paperwork.

One answer is for managers to actively reduce paperwork by questioning every form, requisition, and request for documentation. For example, a supervisor should always try to answer correspondence and memos with phone calls or personal contact. Don't call meetings unless there is a need. Don't attend purposeless meetings; leave early if meetings are not properly organized or run. Cut down on needless travel. Question every trip as if the money were coming out of your own salary. I've tried all of these and saved enough time to implement some of the concepts I espoused as a scientist--though I still have a long way to go. One approach is to defer all technical reading to the early morning hours or to the evenings. There are fewer interruptions and such a schedule frees up daytime hours to interact with the scientists.

Basic Individual Needs

According to Maslow, there are five essential needs--physiological, safety, love, esteem, self-fulfillment--which are in hierarchial progression; each is felt, and can be fulfilled, only after the one below it has, to a large extent, been fulfilled (6). An individual who is struggling desperately to make ends meet must be primarily concerned with basic physiological and safety needs, while a world-renowned scientist, whose accomplishments have been praised and who holds a comfortable position in life, is primarily concerned with efforts aimed at self-fulfillment. The scientist new to the world of work, on the other hand--one who is earning a good salary but is not known in his field--will likely be mostly concerned with self-esteem. If a period of severe economic depression should suddenly occur and both scientists were to lose their jobs, the chief concern of both would very likely shift just as suddenly to the level of basic survival and safety.

Of course it's never that simple, and it is important to remember that the individual's motivation will be influenced to one degree or another, by all of these needs that Maslow has identified. (It's worth noting, by the way, that the one reason money is such a strong motivator is because with it people can, to a large extent, fulfill the three lower level needs.)

Naturally, people don't go around consciously thinking, "Well, I might lose my job so I am now motivated by the lower needs." But an awareness that all people are different and act from different needs--needs that shift in focus and vary in degree--can be a useful tool to the supervisor. The needs, or concerns, of employees will be reflected in their general attitudes and behavior, and the supervisor will need to tailor his style and approach to supervision accordingly.

How does the supervisor go about fulfilling the needs of his scientists? Obviously, before the supervisor can fulfill a need, he must be aware that it exists. The awareness is not always easy to attain, because the employee may not always recognize what is really bothering him. The supervisor must discuss it with him, paying special attention to his failure to mention things he would normally say.

If he is hesitant to talk, it may be because of fear or mistrust. Breaking down such a barrier to open discussion may take time and patience, especially if the style of management has tended to be autocratic or bureaucratic. The employee may be confused by a sudden show of interest and probably will be suspicious of first offers to talk. Once the necessary mutual trust has been developed, his needs can be determined and an attempt can be made to fulfill them. The very fact that the supervisor shows concern will act as a powerful motivating force in increasing his productivity.

The importance of fulfilling individual needs is succinctly put by Masterson and Mara: "Steps such as giving employees feedback on their performance levels and helping them to satisfy their higher needs for status, recognition, prestige, and self-fulfillment on the job must be taken regularly, not sporadically" (7).

Reflections:

Maslow's definition of the five essential needs is still applicable. But as pointed out, everyone is at a different stage of fulfilling his individual needs; thus the supervisor has a difficult task of identifying these various levels. Especially as things such as inflation, world conditions, and political pressures continuously change, even reasonably stable institutions have difficulty. Dealing with these problems is one of the manager's ever-present activities and some problems may have a direct effect on the survival of the organization.

Physical and Technical Support

One of the supervisor's prime responsibilities is to remove roadblocks to research so that scientists can solve technical problems. One important way to do this is to provide adequate physical and technical support. Though many people believe that creative scientists like Edison succeeded without equipment or facilities, exactly the opposite is true. A visit to Greenfield Village in Dearborn, Michigan, provides a glimpse of the range of facilities and equipment available to Edison, including more than one laboratory, chemicals, machinery, and other equipment. He even had a pipe organ, which was used for wind-and-sound experiments and enjoyment.

However, indiscriminate use of funds to satisfy individual whims is not advocated. There are other, more economical avenues a supervisor can take to provide support. Programmable desk calculators and plotters, time-sharing computers, closed-circuit TV, all increase the efficiency of scientists without adding large support groups. Use of support groups on a contractual basis with a university can also pay large dividends, especially in such fields as instrumentation, and computer programming. As Raudsepp points out,

"Although good working conditions and the availability of adequate facilities are not, according to most surveys, the major factors in job satisfaction, the company that provides its technical professionals with modern laboratories, up-to-date equipment, and ample working space undoubtedly has the advantage over the firm that crowds them into tiny work areas and provides them with obsolescent equipment. The 'bull-pen' concept should be totally discarded. How many companies would expect their top executives to function working elbow to elbow with a dozen other executives in a barn-like room? Obviously none; yet the practice of lumping a host of creative technical professionals together and expecting them to produce is still widely prevalent in industry" (8).

How prevalent this practice still is, is not known. However, it has been observed that this problem exists not so much on a bull-pen basis as in the crowding of two or three scientists into small offices made for one. Granted, there are space limitations in most organizations, and most employees will accept, with an explanation, reasonable allocation of available space. Obvious misapportionment of that space is the problem.

To maintain effective control, some organizations group scientists, as far as office and laboratory space is concerned, according to administrative divisions. This is a good idea, provided functional lines parallel administrative lines, but if adequate office or laboratory space exists in fairly remote locations it should be used in preference to arbitrarily overcrowding staff in a limited area under the pretext of efficiency.

Because of his experience and contacts, the supervisor should help scientists make arrangements with the specialists they need to solve their problems. The dominant attitude should be one of working together to solve the problem as quickly and economically as possible.

Reflections:

The supervisor's role in removing roadblocks to research remains as important as before. Unfortunately many supervisors spend time doing just the opposite-- building roadblocks. Providing adequate physical and technical support is still a major responsibility of the supervisor. This is always difficult with tight budgets and the strong tendency to build kingdoms by hiring more people rather than using the same money to maximize the effectiveness of the existing staff.

There are also differences in management attitude. One approach is to hire a lot of people and attack the problem and forget the individual. The other is to hire a minimum staff and work with them to solve the problem, but also use the money saved from salaries to properly support the scientists. The second approach is what I prefer.

In essence, if you cannot properly support a new scientist, it is probably better not to hire one.

Support services are just what the title implies--support-- and within the organization there is always conflict between the operating units and support staff. The support people always feel they aren't appreciated and the operating units feel the support groups are not responsive and so the battle goes. After watching this activity for years it became obvious that both sides are right in their feelings but that the operating units must prevail. In fact, if they do not, the organization will fold, taking the support jobs with it. Some observations:

--If support groups are nonresponsive, competent operating units will bypass them and get their work done outside the organization. This is costly since the organization is, in effect, paying twice for the service.

--The productive staff will provide their own support services. This is more than doubly costly because the higher-paid people hired to do research are doing support work.

--Some research staffs will do their work without proper support services so the research is not done properly.

--Management will ultimately eliminate those support services that decide not to perform.

Thus the message is clear, support services need to perform and do their job of making the organization more efficient or they risk elimination.

However, I don't believe this conflict need exist. What has to be done is to provide only in-house support services that are cost-effective and then treat them as equals, and provide all other support services outside the organization but with ready access. It can work, but the supervisor has to constantly battle the empire builders in the organization.

Part of good support is to provide a scientist with a technician to carry out the routine work. Whether he should be assigned directly to the scientist or operate out of a pool can lead to endless meetings, discussions, and studies. I have operated with both systems, seen both succeed, and both fail. From a theoretical standpoint the pooled approach is more efficient if the criterion is to keep everyone busy, but if the criterion is development of in-depth support for a scientist in a specific field, then the individual assignment is preferred.

The biggest problem with the individual assignment is the inability of many scientists to keep the technician productive. My conclusion is to provide individual support but not on a full-time, permanent basis until the scientist demonstrates the ability to handle the technician. This can best be done by making the first assignment temporary and possibly part-time with close management review.

I said it before and I say it again, "A manager's job is to SUPPORT the scientists", not create roadblocks. In fact, good managers spend a lot of their time removing roadblocks that bureaucrats have created to protect their kingdoms. A supervisor must be prepared for a continuous battle, because there are more incompetent, non-productive, activity-oriented managers than there are those who want to get the job done and accomplish something.

Top Management's Role

Top management's responsibility is to adopt the same attitude advocated here for line supervisors. However, top management should also make sure that middle management supervisors concur that creative thinking is desirable in their departments, and that the supervisors are properly trained to manage creative people. Many of the problems of creating an ideal environment are traceable to middle-management supervisors who do not know how to manage scientists for creative productivity owing to a lack of training; who simply refuse to change their old habits of management; or who just don't know what top management's attitude is toward proper management concepts. To correct the latter situation, top management should take the lead and demonstrate the type of management it expects of its middle-level supervisors.

The makeup of top management is another aspect that should be considered. Who occupies the seats at the oval table? All ex-salesmen, or all ex-business administrators, or all ex-scientists? Hopefully not. Today's problems require answers that can best be made by a balanced top management team. The lawyer, scientist, production manager, salesman, business administrator, marketing manager, financier--all are needed and all should be recognized as professionals in their own fields.

Reflections:

Top management must set an example for their managers, supervisors, and scientists. This example-setting runs the whole gamut from management style to minor aspects such as following the work rules that management sets themselves. The day of "do as I say, not as I do" is gone, and top management must be responsible.

One major role of top management is to foster application of innovative concepts and developments. This can only be accomplished if managers remove the disadvantage of risk-taking. At the present, it is generally safer if a supervisor not try anything new if his operation is going smoothly. The concept of "if it ain't broke, don't fix it" really applies, especially if failure of an innovative improvement could lead to the supervisor's removal.

The goal should be company success rather than division success. Yet, the profit center motive is used by many companies. Thus, if the division is making a profit and the company is just surviving, there is little incentive for the division to institute a new method that might lower its own profits but significantly improve the company picture. The rewards have to support top management's goals or they are not going to see improvement.

Decision-Making

If top management can't make decisions, they can't manage, yet there are a surprising number of so-called managers who survive. One reason for this is that all decisions are not equal, and how fast a decision is implemented is important.

Decisions vary in their nature. Many decisions will enjoy the support of the majority of the employees (80-20 type); these are the easy decisions. The tough ones are the 49-51 splits, for which there is a good possibility that the decision is wrong. A good manager will still make the difficult decision; a poor one will not.

The second aspect of decision-making is how fast the decision is carried out. If there is a long delay, there is a perceived notion that the decision has not been made or the manager has no clout. This perception of power has a significant impact on how effective a manager is. In fact I would say that the perception of power is many times more important than the wielding of real power because people are much more affected by perceptions than by reality.

Committees vs Individual Leadership

Another way to manage is by using committees, but I feel that committees are the bane of most organizations:

--They are misused.
--They are time-consuming.
--They are often ineffective.
--They are a handy excuse for not getting things done.

And the list could go on.

However, they are great if the manager wants to duck responsibility or needs to delay action. Quite frankly, in the real world there are occasions when this latter activity is appropriate, but they should be rather infrequent.

One of the few times a committee is appropriate is when a subject needs study or comment from a variety of viewpoints to help management make a good decision.

Substituting a committee for making management decisions is a mistake. What makes things happen and succeed are entrepreneurial leaders with vision and persistence, who can make decisions. The purpose of an organization is to help the leader accomplish her goals and fulfill her vision efficiently. When the organization ceases to enhance this efficiency, a major overhaul of the organization is in order and probably the first thing to do is get rid of a lot of ineffective committees.

MBO and other Management Methods

MBO, Matrix Management, Demming, etc. have all been tried but often have failed. This is tragic because each of these management methods is the product of some excellent thinking and has the potential of significantly helping an organization. The problem with all of these methods is that the TOP management has to actively embrace the concept and change the rules to allow it to work. Anything less will doom the program to just another exercise in frustration for the middle managers, supervisors, and employees.

Another major problem is the application of a given management method in areas where it does not fit. For example, MBO was aimed at the business community, so when it was applied to the non-profit sector, modifications had to be made. In fact, McConkey wrote a book aimed just at non-profit organizations (9). But the problem doesn't end there. We tried to apply MBO to a research organization and found after we had completed the course that the concept had never been successfully applied to a research environment and if we wanted to be "guinea pigs", we should give it a try. We opted out.

If a new management program is going to be introduced in your organization be sure you have:

--Total commitment from the top.
--First-hand knowledge of where the program has been successfully applied.
--Knowledge that it fits your organization.
--The funds to support it.

Drucker (1974) said it very well, "In the traditional managerial organization such as management texts discuss, top management is final judge. This means, in effect that management's most important power is the veto power, and its most important role is to say no to proposals and ideas that are not completely thought through and worked out. This concept is caricatured in that well-known jingle composed many years ago by a senior Unilever executive,

Along this tree
From root to crown
Ideas flow up
And vetoes down.

In the innovative organization, the first and most important job of management is the opposite: It is to convert impractical, half-baked, and wild ideas into concrete innovative reality. In the innovative organization, top management sees it as its job to listen to ideas and to take them seriously. Top management, in the innovative organization, knows that new ideas are always 'impractical'."

4

The Magic Keys: Communication and Recognition

1974 "The Scientist Observes"

The ability to communicate effectively is perhaps the skill most often lacking in scientific supervision. When the dust has settled after a fiasco in any organization, research or otherwise, poor communication comes through as the cause.

Roethlisberger outlined two schools of thought on communication:

"One school assumes that communication between A and B, for example, has failed when B does not accept what A has to say as being fact, true, or valid, and that the goal of communication is to get B to agree with A's opinions, ideas, facts, or information.

The position of the other school of thought is quite different. It assumes that communication has failed when B does not feel free to express his feelings to A because B fears they will not be accepted by A. Communications is facilitated when on the part of A or B or both there is a willingness to express and accept differences" (1).

This last condition must prevail for open communication to be effective. An atmosphere of fear has no place in an organization concerned with creative research.

1988 "The Manager Reflects"

Reflections:

A supervisor's inability to communicate effectively is so obvious and the extent of such problems has been heard so many times, that it is often dismissed out of hand. But for an ideal environment to ever have a chance of existing, effective communication is essential.

Of course, poor written communications can hinder a career, but in general writing is so poor that most companies have someone on their staff to clean up the written reports that go outside the company and all journals have editors to filter out the duds.

The need for the ability to talk to one another is also important and this open one-on-one communication as previously described is essential to successful research.

But oral communication before a group--that is something different. The lack of oral communication skills can negatively affect one's career, and in some cases kill it. There you are, stark naked, in front of not only your peers but your boss and the people who work for you. If you bomb, everyone gets a piece of the flack and your reputation is affected. The odds are really against you:

--This is it; you're on stage; no rewrites are possible.
--Murphy's Law is at its best:

  a. The mike fails.
  b. The projector jams.

c. There are seven wrong ways to put a slide in a projector.
d. There is not enough light to read your notes.
e. Your last experiment doesn't support your two years of data.
f. Your mouth is dry and your knees are shaking.

Yet this had better be good or else!   Overstated? Unfortunately, not really.

No matter what the occasion, you don't know who may be in your audience or why. When I was looking for possible employees I sought out a chance to hear him or her speak and I didn't care what the subject was. When I evaluated my staff, I had everyone of them present their research orally. I was not only interested in the research but how it was presented. On unannounced occasions, the Director would sit in on the presentations. This may have been the only time the Director had seen this person perform and thus he probably formed a mental picture.

What I have observed over the years is that managers carry an image of every employee in their heads. Surprisingly, some managers may not know an employee in another section personally but still carry an image of them based on second-hand feedback from other managers on the staff. Thus, when an employee gives a talk, her image and reputation are on the line, perhaps to a greater extent than she realizes.

It is almost impossible to argue a poor mental picture from the boss's mind without another experience that will erase the old one. I wish I were overstating this situation but I am not. If we simply think of the people we have met just once, we know we form a mental picture based on just as shallow a set of criteria, if not worse--like dress, haircut, what they do, who they are married to or if they are single, etc.

The supervisor's perception of your ability to communicate is often the only measure he has of your performance.

"So Do An Outstanding Job"

This is human nature and thus we have to deal with it. If you want to get ahead, you must learn how to effectively communicate.

Scientist to Scientist

It was once possible for a single person to be adequately knowledgeable in many disciplines; unfortunately, that day is past, because of the fantastic knowledge explosion. Today, as a scientist attempts to solve a problem creatively, he must rely on other scientists skilled in specific disciplines, particularly when time is critical.

The scientist must be able to relate to his resource people; but the greater the difference in background, the greater the communication gap can be--a gap further widened by the proliferation of specialized languages, symbols, or notations, particularly when the same notation means two different things in two different disciplines.

An effective supervisor can help his scientists bridge the communications gap in several ways. He can encourage them to take advantage of short courses in their own and allied fields. He can suggest participation in seminars, reading outside their field, participation in technical meetings, formal courses, part-time appointments in allied fields, and sabbaticals.

The supervisor should promote scientist-scientist interaction by recognizing the positive effect that contact between colleagues has on creative productivity. As Pelz and Andrews found in their extensive studies, "For both Ph.D. groups and the engineers, the more time a man spent contacting his colleagues (up to a point), the higher his performance. The optimum time for Ph.D.'s seemed to be somewhere between six and ten hours a week per colleague (very few indicated amounts greater then these); the optimum for engineers was slightly higher, somewhere between eight and fifteen hours a week per colleague. In all three groups, the scientists who performed at the highest levels spent considerably more time communicating with their colleagues than was typical for their group" (2).

Reflections:

Another way to increase the scientist-to-scientist communication is to set up roundtables or seminars in which the scientists discuss their research by giving a short formal presentation to their peers and then having open discussion.

Joint studies between scientists are also encouraged where they have each demonstrated ability to conduct independent research.

I would also re-emphasize the findings of Pelz and Andrews. The most productive scientists are those who communicate frequently with their colleagues. A supervisor's job is to encourage this interaction.

Supervisor to Scientist

This is a tough area. Much depends on the management style adopted by the supervisor. If it is autocratic, the communications will consist primarily of giving orders and receiving little honest feedback. Discussion will be tailored to what the scientist thinks the 'boss' wants to hear, and the 'boss' will reward this behavior. The autocratic supervisor will tend to brand as 'troublemakers' or undesirable employees those who express a differing opinion. Creativity has little chance under these conditions.

An autocratic system of management promotes fear and rigidity in an organization. On the surface everything appears well-organized and the organization runs smoothly. Nobody rocks the boat, because employees never question procedures; but creativity is effectively inhibited.

Threats are used in some organizations, often quite effectively, to get good short-term results; over the long run, however, this practice destroys the organization or at least eliminates most innovation.

A participative form of organization will lead to true creative productivity. Completely open discussions and candor between supervisor and scientist are essential. Problems should be openly discussed, not in the context of employer-employee, but in the spirit of, "How can we best solve this problem by working together to accomplish the objectives of the organization?"

Open discussion and candor are particularly difficult if the supervisor must constructively discipline a scientist, and yet this is an important area. Unfortunately, many supervisors do not recognize how vital constructive criticism is, or do not know how to give it. If a supervisor feels a need for additional information in this area, books by Feinberg (3) and Raudsepp (4) can be of considerable help.

Reflections:

After participating in and observing communications at all levels, it appears the thing that is generally missing is constructive candor. It is amazing how many supervisors prefer not to level with employees and then wonder why they have continuing problems. The poor performer who has not been told by his previous supervisor what the problems are can be a difficult problem for a new supervisor. Furthermore, if a new supervisor ducks these initial responsibilities in the first year as a supervisor, it will become very difficult to deal effectively with the poor performer. Probably the most difficult task is to discuss anything with an employee who requires disciplinary action. According to the literature, this can be solved by focusing on the actions of the employee rather than the employee himself. While I agree with this, I have not found the task either easy or pleasant. Presently, it appears that jointly established, reasonable performance standards help establish an objective basis for constructive discussions.

Top Management to Scientist

One of the concerns of top management is, or should be, the lack of effective ways to determine the real questions that face the scientist. Staff meetings with supervisors yield plenty of questions, but they don't seem to be the real ones. In fact, they usually are not. Why not? Primarily because of poor communications.

The meetings and discussions ought to result in real communication but, in most cases, they are actually discussions of screened information. This is particularly true if the style of middle management tends to be autocratic. Everyone up and down the line has been hearing only what he wants to hear, and an honest concern has little chance of emerging.

Does top management really want the truth? In most instances it actually does. When profits, productivity, morale, or other aspects really get bad and it decides to do something about improving communications, several predictable things are usually done.

First, the 'open door policy' is established or dusted off, since many organizations have had such a policy for years. This policy, which theoretically allows any employee to speak confidentially with any manager, is excellent, but in practice it usually doesn't work. Unfortunately, the only individuals who take advantage of the policy are those who already are on friendly terms with the supervisor or the very few who are willing to lay their jobs on the line. Occasionally someone will drop in with a small problem, but the gut issues will not be forthcoming.

Assured, despite the facts, that the 'open door policy' has improved communications considerably, an organization embarking on a communications program then takes another step and initiates a program of employee meetings.

These meetings are a very good communications tool for presenting the management view of questions that affect all employees, or large numbers of employees. They serve well to provide information direct from top management, eliminating the distortion and confusion that occur when facts filter through the chain of command. However, they are by their very nature a one-way kind of communication. The formal meeting with large groups seldom results in any penetrating questions and provides little feedback as to what the employees really think. After an appropriate period of time, the whole communications program is deemed a success, a report is filed, and the whole subject is dropped.

Another approach is to set up a task force of low-level employees to study the organization and make constructive recommendations to top management on ways to improve it. This will provide some valuable guidelines if the head of the organization is sincerely interested, sets it up himself, selects the right people, and grants immunity from disciplinary action for what they might report to him. This group will need to meet frequently and for a considerable amount of time, perhaps two hours a week for six months to a year. Much additional time will be spent by individual members in discussions with other employees in an attempt to get at the real, underlying problems.

It should be recognized by all concerned that many of the problems brought to management's attention will not be solved instantly when the task force has done its work. Reasonable employees will understand and accept this. To them the important thing is progress by management in trying to solve the problems. This approach may not be perfect but it will help top management get some idea of what their real problems are.

Another method that will help identify the real problems is for middle and top management people to come out of their offices and meet regularly with individual scientists on a one-to-one basis. A different man can be scheduled each week if a schedule is necessary.

How should one proceed? Well, one way is to seek out the man and discuss his work with him. Try to find out if outside factors are slowing him up and frustrating attempts to accomplish the mission. This will take some time, but probably not as much time as the meetings and task forces that have to be set up to straighten out messes created because top management didn't know what was really going on.

A lot of listening is necessary during these personal meetings, and critical comments should be avoided unless something obvious--such as safety--is involved, even if the manager disagrees with much the scientist says. During these visits the manager should be gaining an insight into problems that exist in the organization, and not trying to solve every one on the spot. Once they are identified, the problems can and should be dealt with through normal channels. The organizational chain should be respected as far as negative aspects are concerned, but ignored when praise is sincerely deserved and honestly given. It should be remembered that these visits are not formal inspection trips.

If top management shows a sincere interest in what the scientist is doing, the areas in which the organization is functioning smoothly, as well as the complaints, will come forth naturally. Unfortunately there are always a few habitual gripers in any organization and the manager probably should ignore much of what they say. However, all real concerns should be discussed with the employee's supervisor and corrected if valid; and, of course, the employee should remain anonymous.

When the manager starts to hear the same complaint from a number of individuals, he is obviously dealing with a problem that is more than a personal gripe. It should be listened to seriously, discussed with the management staff, and corrected if possible--or at least the situation should be explained to the scientist. Many problems stem from misinformation getting to employees through poor communications. When this happens, and it happens often, they should be given the truth as soon as possible.

What has been outlined requires work on management's part, but should produce great dividends in creative research and productivity.

Reflections:

My years in management have shown me that the difficulty of management communicating with the scientist is greater than I had anticipated as a scientist. As a project leader--an immediate supervisor--I found it not so hard, but as a manager, I found that the total number of people who need contact tends to make it very difficult. For a manager, that sounds like a good excuse; I still reject it and will continue to strive to keep the direct lines open.

Also, my earlier suggestion that the organizational chain should be ignored when praise is sincerely deserved and honestly given can lead to some awkward situations. For example, I applied this approach to an employee who had done a good job on a specific project under my control. I happened along while he was finishing up the work and on the spot gave him some sincere and honest praise, and followed it up with a letter to his supervisor with a carbon copy to him. This latter action was a real mistake as he was then being reprimanded for poor work on other projects and abuse of work hours. My letter created lots of problems for his supervisor. If I had just complimented him on his specific accomplishments on my project and just notified his supervisor, everything would have worked out; but as it was, my jumping the chain with a copy of my letter to him undercut the supervisor's position. I didn't stop my compliments for work well done, but I did stop sending letters directly to employees.

Recognition is Vital

If the supervisor has created the type of environment described so far, creative research will follow. So one might ask, "Why is anything else needed?"

In fact a great deal more is needed, because there are many problems to solve, not one or two. To ensure continued creative work, appropriate recognition must be given for past success. Poor work , on the other hand, should be closely followed by constructive criticism, as has already been stated. Though difficult, it is essential, because every scientist needs to know where he stands with management.

Much has been written on the importance of recognition. For example, the Federal Council for Science and Technology found that four out of the top ten most important factors in an environment for quality dealt with recognition (5). The U.S. Department of Health, Education, and Welfare found that four of the eleven factors that influence an environment for science dealt with need for some form of recognition (6). Raudsepp stated,

"Personal recognition from peers, from supervisors and management in all its forms, is one of the most important incentives. Yet it is this one area that is most neglected in industry. Most recent studies show that not only is inadequate personal recognition given for individual achievement, there is also a wide divergence of opinion between technical professionals and managerial personnel on what constitutes the proper method of recognition. Since recognition of the scientists' and engineers' contributions is so tremendously important to them, failure on the part of management and supervision to provide adequate recognition can seriously undermine morale (7)."

With so much agreement that recognition is a vital factor in a creative research environment, it is shocking to see how many organizations put very little emphasis upon it.

Reflections:

A major way to give scientists recognition is to be sure they have the opportunity and support to work on real, significant problems. Then when problems are successfully solved, the scientists should be given awards by their peer organizations and promotions and/ or bonuses.

Although I still agree with this section, I would like to add that a similar problem exists regarding lack of recognition for good supervisors. Probably the biggest deterrent to good supervision is that proper recognition is not given to the good supervisor and the poor one continues to create ever-growing problems for the supervisor who follows.

The lack of proper rewards for good supervision is complicated by the fact that what is proper is really not straight-forward. Some supervisors respond to perks like a new office, title, or parking space; others, to higher pay. But regardless of the type of reward, there is still a question as to whether it is sufficient to really motivate a person to be a good supervisor. As wage compression continues, paperwork increases, and personnel restrictions become complex, there is some question as to who will even be willing to become a supervisor, let alone desire to be a good one. This area needs much attention given the new constraints found in business today. Of course, one solution is to return to straight authoritative control in which the employee's sensitivity is completely ignored. I reject this solution.

A major way to give supervisors recognition is to allow them to set their own hours and give them more control over budget and personnel. This may sound simple but most organizations will reject these options. Such a rejection is unfortunate.

Emphasis on quality is another major form of recognition, from top management on down. Most employees take personal pride in doing a good job. If a supervisor encourages quality and recognizes it, everyone will benefit.

Quality is free--but only over the long term. Over the short term, quality is very expensive. Thus the only quality programs that really work are those to which TOP management is committed. This means that they have to look beyond the quarterly bottom line. I've listened to many talks on quality and have read Demming's and Crosby's books; they are excellent, but I still don't see the application in very many organizations. The rhetoric is there but the real substance is missing: Get the product out; exceed the quota; we don't have time for quality; "bug off" you guys in the white coats.

The only quality programs I know of that have been successful are those in which the CEO insists on it and provides the means and support to see that it is done.

A story of what it takes comes from a company that produced a fabricated product that had to meet a specific strength value for acceptance. The product was made, evaluated, and found to be 2 lbs. below the required 168 lbs. strength required. The question was, "Do we ship the material?" It was less than 2% below specification and it took a significant amount of time and money to make the product. The debate raged. The quality control person said it shouldn't be shipped. Production said yes, marketing said yes, shipping was neutral, and sales were for it. Finally the controversy got to the CEO. He listened to the facts in the situation and then called a meeting on the loading dock with everyone from the plant assembled. He reviewed the situation and emphasized that the material was less than 2% below the accepted standard. He did not make a long-winded speech on the importance of quality, he did not look to blame other suppliers of materials used in their product--a common ploy. What he did say was brilliant: "Scrap it." The message was concise and understood by all. "We only ship quality." That decision cost the company a lot of money that day--quality is expensive over the short term--but it saved the company over the long term because it ensured its competitiveness by putting out a known, reliable product. It saved the company thousands of dollars in hype, quality control programs, quality inspectors, etc. The message was clear: "Quality is everyone's responsibility. If anyone lets down we all suffer and the result of that is we all face losing our job."

The CEO let every employee know that he valued quality in the product and in the production. He was stating his belief in the employees' pride and performance. And whereas he caused them extra work, he was also recognizing their usual high-quality performance by maintaining a clear standard.

No matter how you package it, quality starts at the TOP

How to Give Recognition

The forms of recognition are many. Authorship of papers, promotions, new equipment, stock options, bonuses, pay increases, public acclaim, cash awards, trips, certificates, a pat on the back by a fellow scientist or supervisor, the mere demonstration of confidence by a supervisor who selects the scientist to represent the organization at a meeting, are all effective recognition; but the degree of effectiveness depends on the person and the circumstances.

As important as the need to give recognition is the actual manner in which the recognition is given. Above all, it must be given sincerely.

Presenting the certificate or cash award and conveying by one's attitude that it's just another administrative detail will effectively undermine the motivational benefits of the recognition. Such awards are known to have been mailed to the employee, and in one instance it was presented in the men's room. Ridiculous yes, and obviously this type of behavior by supervisors has produced negative motivational effect. If the organization has a good incentive awards program but isn't motivating the scientists, the method by which the awards are given is probably the explanation.

Another area that creates real problems with any recognition program is the mis-selection of the proper award. As an example, take two employees: one an average man who one day comes up with a successful solution to an important problem, the other a man who consistently works above his present job requirements. Given the choice of a cash award and pay raise, which man should receive which award to produce maximum creative productivity? To the employee it makes sense to give the cash award to the man who has solved the single problem and the pay raise to the man who is consistently working above his job requirements. Now, to many supervisors this also makes sense; but some do just the opposite.

We don't know why, but this situation is not unique and it is interesting to consider how some employees react to this reversal. First, the average employee who received the raise may well be deluded into thinking that his overall performance is very good and so is not motivated to improve his performance. The above-average employee, though momentarily pleased with the cash award, will shortly feel cheated and lose some respect for management. Nor does this incident end here; the employee's co-workers also react to this situation in many ways. Some may be indifferent, some concerned, but many will be demotivated by what they consider poor judgment by management. They reason: "Why knock myself out, it sure didn't pay off for so-and-so." Of course, these reactions are over-simplified and many others will occur, but the point is that it is not adequate just to have an award or other incentive program; how it is implemented and administered is equally important.

Mere presentation of a challenging situation can be a powerful motivator for some individuals, but successful solution must be followed by proper recognition. One of a supervisor's jobs is to decide what is proper recognition.

Reflections:

Awards--Oh, to have the wisdom of Solomon!

This is a most vexing subject to deal with. The manager is almost always wrong when awards are given--even when they come from outside the organization, the managers are still blamed for lousy choices. You either give too many, not enough, or always to the wrong people. The monetary value is too much or too little, and the highest-paid people always get the largest amounts.

I talked to one employee who had received three awards in four years and he complained bitterly that no one appreciated his work, and so it goes. In fact, at a meeting at which an expert on motivation was speaking, I took the occasion to ask him how one would set up an effective awards program. His immediate answer was to do what one of the big successful companies does and give 80% of all employees some kind of award every year.

Even if one solves the problem of who should get the recognition, there is the question of how it should be presented:

--One-on-one: Supervisor to employee or Manager to
  employee.
--Group or section meeting and person singled out.
--Private meeting of all those to be recognized.
--A company-wide awards meeting.

The list of options goes on. Having observed all of these methods, I do not find any one of them a standout. However, if your purpose is to motivate the staff, then the company-wide meeting is better because (if you made good selections) everyone will be a witness. However, the awards ceremony attendance should be voluntary, and not everyone will agree that the best people received awards.

I tried very hard to reward my best producers as often as possible and with the largest amounts possible--and I still didn't feel that everyone got what they deserved. The only thing that helped was that my staff knew that they were top notch and I took every occasion I could to reinforce that.

Jewkes, Thompson and Dalton (1979) observed that, "if you can successfully build your reward system around meeting trivial deadlines, filling out endless reports, and strictly quantifiable criteria, you'll never have to worry about creativity again" (8).

Giving Credit Where it is Due

Ideas are the mainstay of the creative individual. His function is to produce new concepts and techniques, and understandably attaches great value to recognition for his ideas. Yet a surprising number of supervisors are inclined to present new ideas to management as their own, or as though they mysteriously flowed from the project or section without origination by a human being. This reprehensible practice not only leads scientists to be cautious about advancing new ideas, it may actually cause them to stop their creative thought processes. They see little value in advancing the image of the supervisor by their contributions, without proper recognition for themselves.

Certainly a supervisor should be encouraged to develop and advance his own ideas, but much greater progress is made in attacking problems when he encourages, advances, and credits ideas conceived by individuals in the project. If a supervisor's techniques do not include consistently giving scientists credit for good creative work, he is destroying creativity and doing a poor supervisory job.

Reflections:

Plagiarism is something that is considered unethical, and yet not giving due credit is a fault we all share to one degree or another. This is particularly true of those who work on patentable ideas. It is often almost impossible to determine exactly who contributed to a creative idea. But that is not generally a major problem for managers. The major problem is supervisors or other scientists who use others' ideas as their own and will not give due credit for them.

Good, constant communication with scientists will acquaint the supervisor with the individual scientists' work, and can allow the supervisor to determine more about the likely source of ideas.

5

The Sticky Wickets

The following subjects, listed in alphabetical order, are REFLECTIONS I have had on other areas I have discovered since becoming a manager. The fact that it is lengthy points out a major difference between my view as a scientist and that as a manager. Also, I should point out that I have included discussion of some items that are not generally included in management courses. I hope my candor is both refreshing and interesting, but most of all helpful to other managers. Progress in effective management will not be made if we continue to insist on relearning the basics.

Activity vs Accomplishment

Discerning the difference between activity and accomplishment is so central and so important that I want to emphasize it. Most managers, supervisors, and many scientists are very busy with activity--whereas the focus should be on accomplishment. For example:

--Producing reports based on time--weekly, monthly, quarterly. What is more important is how many high-quality reports were published this year.

--Meeting an arbitrary deadline and time schedule for performance reviews. Rather, it is more important how many career development plans were completed, promotions and awards received, and obstacles overcome.

--Attending some minimum number of EEO meetings. More important is giving minorities every opportunity for hiring, training, and promotions.

--Hosting some number of visitors or answering some number of inquiries. Rather, more significantly, what specific problems did you help solve?

The list could go on but I'm sure the point is clear. My real concern is whether or not managers have the courage to get rid of activity and concentrate on accomplishments.

Adverse Situations

We all have to handle adverse situations in our lives, and how we handle them probably tells the world more about us than any of our other actions. How do you react when your performance rating is lower than you feel it should be? What about denial of a pay raise or loss of a promotion you thought you deserved? Or a transfer you don't want? One reaction is anger. Don't indulge yourself; it could be career damaging. When a personnel action is taken, such as a transfer, management is focused on you--you are being transferred due to their action. If you accept it and do your best, you'll be viewed as a team player. If you fight it, you will be viewed as a troublemaker.

Let me tell you a not-so-secret: Troublemakers lose. Oh, they win some battles or technicalities, even court actions; but career-wise they lose. I don't say this to intimidate employees or supervisors but rather to be honest and let you know that managers have enough problems that they won't tolerate troublemakers for long. It isn't so much a personal matter as one of conservation of limited energy. Troublemakers burn a lot of management energy and a company can't afford it.

Now let me differentiate between a troublemaker and a concerned employee. A concerned employee can and will be just as vocal as the troublemaker but her focus is different. The troublemaker focuses on her own problems and well-being whereas a concerned employee focuses on actions that adversely affect the company. The concern may be some personnel practice and thus the same as that of the troublemaker but the focus is company concern not just self. If an employee really believes she has been unjustly treated she should appeal the action to a higher level and do it in a professional manner.

Budget Problems.

Budgets are something that scientists grouse about and administrators deal with. This subject has gained greater importance recently due to fiscal cutbacks. What has happened is that more scientists have to compete for the limited research dollars available. If one equates business and research, this turn of events is considered good; however, if one is interested in true creative research, I doubt that this is the way to go.

To effectively compete for funds, the scientist has to propose a solution to a problem, give minute details of methodology, etc. The creativity is seriously dampened, and what remains is a proof of concept or demonstration of an idea. Thus when the scientist is funded for the demonstration work, he hopefully can squeeze out a little original research so he has another guaranteed success to submit on the next go-around. The system works in terms of activity but a substantial amount of the time of the creative scientist is spent writing proposals, soliciting funds, and preparing reports, and unfortunately a lot of this is wasted time.

A better approach is for management and senior scientists to determine the real, significant problems and then let the scientists do their thing and management provide the funds and proper environment.

One of the major reasons some organizations are in financial trouble is that the only incentive given its manager regarding budgets is to spend them. Their chief mode of operation is to never return the money; to return the money is to admit all sorts of fallibilities--you can't plan, your program flounders, you are not creative, your program is not important, and so it goes. Drucker (1973) pointed this problem out as being characteristic of Russian planning 30 to 40 years ago, "one of its major weaknesses" (1). This narrow view of budgeting is reinforced by a one-year fiscal cycle.

What is needed is not a complete overhaul of the system, but the encouragement of prudent spending by letting the organization carry over unspent funds into the following year. Oh, the bookkeeping is more difficult, but are we in business to make life simple for bookkeepers? Rather, we should focus on accomplishment, not activity.

Computers in Management

With the proliferation of personal computers, it was of interest to me to see if this new tool would improve my management effectiveness. Thus I conducted a one-year study of the use of a PC in the office management situation for a research operation. I identified the many tasks that I was responsible for and that I thought possibly could be handled using a PC. Then I set about applying this new tool. The results were surprising.

The biggest surprise and success was the improvement gained due to review and analysis of my management activities. Instead of computerizing some actions, I eliminated them. Others were modified so that they didn't need a computer and still others turned out to be too big for a personal computer to handle, yet important enough that they were placed on a larger computer.

The word-processing program led to the greatest increase in efficiency. This is not surprising but the time saved alone paid for the whole system. In this respect the use of word processing for reports is particularly desirable because it allows one to rewrite and improve reports without long, expensive retyping.

The most successful application was with the research program, and it was done using the word-processing functions. Simply, the use of the computer allowed me to integrate the organization's goals with the annual project review, study plans, personnel, and budgeting in one document. That in itself was significant, but when an update was necessary the computer allowed me to make relatively small changes and still end up with a professional, complete document. I also admit that this study forced me to review all the individual studies in the research area and that in itself was worth all the time spent.

I also set up a personnel talent data base. My purpose was to have a ready access to who had expertise in what area. This was successful insofar as bringing it on-line, but I found that after inputting all the information, I didn't need the computer to help me, and updating was a problem. This would be great for a new manager especially if she came from outside the organization.

Budget is an area that would have been greatly helped if we were organized in a different manner. However, our financial activities were handled by a central group and they used computers all the time, so for me to set up a second system would have been redundant. But under normal conditions, the computer has really found a niche in this application.

In our laboratory our equipment inventory was already on computer so this application was not necessary for my PC. However, this may be a fertile field for computerization for other laboratories.

Chemicals are similar to equipment; although I attempted to computerize this list, it became too large and thus was placed on a larger computer. It is important to note that although we started out with the idea of getting a good chemical inventory for safety purposes, it was also successful in identifying what chemicals we had in stock and therefore didn't need to purchase. We found that this was a double savings: If we didn't buy additional chemicals, we also didn't have to pay for disposal of excess chemicals.

I concluded that the personal computer is a very useful tool for the effective research manager. Unfortunately, there are many tasks that a manager does that are not computer-oriented, and a lot of time can be wasted trying to make them so. The major questions one should ask are:

--Should I continue to do this task at all?

--How much time will it take to keep the files updated, and is the potential use worth it?

Mentors

Throughout most of my time as a manager, I was an active mentor. Having received the benefits of a mentor myself, I recognize the importance of this role, and I encourage each employee to seek a good mentor. However, one must be aware that this has to be a mutually agreeable situation. You can't just go out and pick a mentor; the relationship has to be mutually developed. Likewise, some scientists reject managers who try to be their mentors.

Opportunity

Familiarity breeds contempt. Well, in management familiarity also breeds inaction. When someone is promoted to supervisor she has one year to establish herself with her employees. After the first performance review if she has not levelled with the problem employees, it will be much more difficult from there on, for then she will become part of the problem. So if a manager has to take negative action, she must lay the groundwork the first year, level with the employee, and if she still has to proceed she can do it in the second year. It is a long time frame, but to be a successful supervisor, one has to be fair and give one's employees time to prove themselves. Obviously, if the employee has committed a criminal offense or a serious breach of conduct, the time frame would be much shorter.

Paperwork

GET RID OF IT!!!

Paperwork is the credo of some managers: If you don't know what to do, ask for a report--weekly, monthly, quarterly, semiannually, yearly--or if you really want to cripple your staff, ask for daily diary reports.

The job of the manager is to get the paperwork monkey off the staff's back. It won't be easy, as most bureaucrats only understand more and more paperwork. In fact one of the cornerstones of research management is the "Quarterly Report". It seems to be dogma that you can't do research unless you prepare quarterly reports. Frankly, I found that I could do without them as a manager, and the reason was simple: The final published report gave me the information I sought both in terms of what the scientist was doing and what he had accomplished. Writing quarterly reports is pure and simply activity, not accomplishment--and that is the bottom line. If the immediate supervisor under my management needed a quarterly report from the scientists for training or accountability purposes, I left that to his discretion. But they all, including the scientists, knew that this paperwork was not a requirement of upper management.

I personally feel that the time spent on all these activity reports is questionable--a much better method is to meet with each of your scientists once a year for an oral presentation of their research, coupled with frequent contact with the scientists in their work areas during the year.

The only written documentation necessary is the study plan, project notebook, data files, published reports, and special reports required by the funding unit. Managers should continually review their needs and eliminate unnecessary reports. That is all we really need if we focus on accomplishment rather than activity in research.

Personal Problems--Or, How Managers Really Earn Their Pay

As a scientist I never really understood why managers always ended up the highest-paid people. In fact, before I became a manager, I went to one and asked him flat out, "What do you do?" After a long pause he answered, "I spend a lot of time meeting with people, just like we're doing now." That sure didn't sound like too big a deal, and at the time, I really believed that 99% of our problems as scientists were due to our managers. Well, after becoming one, I quickly found out that, athough I would be meeting with people, they were not there to make idle conversation. We are talking about helping solve life crisis problems and, since they affect the workplace, the manager gets involved.

Over the course of eight years I have dealt either directly or indirectly with the following problems:

Alcoholism	Mental illness
Battery	Drugs
Incompetence	Sexual harassment
Divorce	Egomania
Exhibitionists	Theft
Major sickness	Heart attacks
Radicalism	And others

In all the courses I took, and reading on management I did, virtually nothing dealt with these problems in a real way. Oh, they quoted chapter and verse of rules and regulations. They handed out brochures, and told funny stories, but this business above was serious. One could look at this list and say, "What kind of an organization were you involved in?" But before you cast too many stones at my organization, check with your own management or personnel section and see how you are. My guess is at least as bad, if not a whole lot worse.

If you have any sensitivity--and to be a good manager you need lots--you will recognize that these are tough, individual problems that require you to be discreet. That is why a scientist doesn't hear about many of the problems. You also need to be knowledgeable, sensitive, firm, and have a strong desire to help your people solve their problems and succeed. If you don't care or are perceived as a manager who doesn't care, your management effectiveness will revert to the basic 'boss-worker' relationship, which is not conducive to good creative research.

The major reason these subjects are rarely dealt with in management courses or books is that each situation is unique and, although there is some similarity, there is a great enough difference that pat answers usually don't work.

Publishing

The primary output of a scientist is a report, and whenever possible it should be published. It is not unreasonable to expect a scientist to produce an average of two significant, top-quality, publishable reports a year. I realize it is questionable to set a number, but I found that by having a reasonable goal I was able to objectively sort out the non-productive staff and was able to identify the outstanding ones. Interestingly, though not surprisingly, most of the complaints about counting publications came from the least productive.

Having said this about publications, my own personal criterion for output was the successful solution of a real, significant problem, and successful solution of a problem included technical, economic, and political acceptance. A real breakthrough is far more important than numbers of publications. Unfortunately, a lot of pseudo-managers find it much easier just to count publications rather than to make the much harder decision of evaluating scientific contributions. Realistically, universities and many other organizations and companies still place great emphasis on numbers, and to help protect the scientists' mobility, it is important to encourage publication of good reports.

Research vs Development vs Technology Transfer

I'm reluctant to tackle this subject since so much has been written on it, but it is important that the subject be discussed in the context of how activity can be substituted for accomplishments. First some definitions:

--Research: The creative solution to problems.

--Development: The steps necessary to take the creative solution and commit it to usefulness.

--Technology Transfer: The dissemination of the creative solution to people or organizations where it can be applied.

Our problem is that we get these three activities mixed up in an organization. We try to 'PERT' chart research, use brainstorming for development, and write action plans for technology transfer. We must recognize the necessity of each step and support the programs and people that foster them. Any organization purporting to do useful research must embrace the interactivity, yet recognize the separativeness and provide appropriate staff to carry out the separate functions. Management may reject tried and true methods of disseminating information because they are not new and are not therefore Technology Transfer. For example, we have had a very successful technology transfer of packaging information through the University of Wisconsin Engineering Department for 18 years. People actually pay for the information. The model is there and proven successful, but does the organization build on the model? No, they prefer to concentrate on new reports and brochures. The point I'm making is that many organizations fail to capitalize on what works but rather are continuing to look for something different on the premise that if it is old it is no good and if it is new it is better--Hogwash!

Research vs Technical Service

One of the conflicts in management is separating research from technical service. In essence, research is concerned with the unknown and the creative solution to problems; technical service is the application of knowledge to the solution of problems. This conflict arises because in industry most companies want technical service, not research. Part of this conflict is due to tax advantages but primarily it is due to the nature of business. Many managers are hired to keep the status quo, certainly not to encourage some employee to come up with a better way to do something. This is especially true if it upsets the present system and if the new idea threatens the in-place capital investment. Now, there is absolutely nothing wrong with this position provided everyone understands it. It is when some employees believe that because they work in the "research department" of the company that the company obviously wants breakthroughs. Check again; the unit called "research department" may in reality be a "technical service department".

An example is a person working for the "research department" of a large paper company. What management generally wants from their research department are ways to make the paper faster, cheaper, or better. This calls for some real research. But if the management just wants the person to apply known techniques and solve specific operating problems the company is really operating a technical service department

As a manager you must be sure you know what you are really managing--a real research organization or technical service group with the title "Research Department." There is nothing inherently good or bad about research or technical service; it is just critical that you as a manager and you as a scientist know who you are really working for and what the real goals of the department are.

Scientist Ego

We each have an ego, but some of us have a pregnant one--and it is the wish of all of us that those who do would deliver soon so we can get along with them.

Scientists are no different; in fact, I think pregnant egos are greater among scientists than people in many other fields.

So, if you buy this thesis, then as a manager how do you live with those insufferable ones and still keep your cool. It is not easy, but if the scientists have really provided solutions to real, significant problems, you must help them crow--they deserve it. That is not the management problem. Rather, it is the incompetent pseudo-scientist, with the list of degrees, inane incomprehensible reports, and a tendency to browbeat others, who is difficult to handle.

Having known a few of those types, I have found a couple of effective solutions:

1. Assign them a real, significant problem. If they are worth a darn, they will accomplish something and then have the right to be a bit insufferable. If they don't, you both will know the truth and then they become less unbearable, leave the organization, or retire.

2. Have a heart-to-heart talk with them in terms of how they are really perceived by others. On some occasions this is successful. No. 1 is almost surefire.

There is nothing wrong with having a little ego; in fact, it is important, especially given the need for self sustainment in the face of multiple failures, which is typical of a good scientist. The problem comes when incompetent ones flaunt their egos based on hollow achievements. I might add that at one time just getting a Ph.D was some justification for a bit of excessive ego, but now with the reduced requirements and the fact that if one has enough time and money almost anyone can get one, it is of little legitimate ego support.

Secretary Utilization

The proper utilization of a secretary may seem off the subject of management of scientists, but in reality a good secretary can be a great asset to the manager. Unfortunately many managers don't know how to work with a secretary, and this isn't surprising. I don't know of any training that a manager gets for effectively working with a secretary. There are lots of courses for secretaries and for managers but few are devoted to bridging the interface effectively. A good secretary can be an extension of the manager. If they are just considered clerk-typists who input information into a word processor or typewriter, a· great loss in management effectiveness is the result.

A good secretary can greatly enhance a manager's success by:

--Providing a sounding board for the manager's ideas. Not every idea a manager has is great. A secretary usually has a much better feel for the typical employee's attitude as a product of her extensive network, which is different from that of the manager.

--Providing critical feedback and rewrite to documents written by the manager.

--Initiating drafts of written documents for the manager.

--Providing continuity of schedule.

--Handling independent projects for the manager such as fact-finding, data formatting, and presentations.

--Providing moral support when things go bad (and many times they do) and sharing information. In essence, a secretary can be a real helpmate.

You will notice I have not listed the normal activities of a stereotypical secretary--not that these activities are not important--but rather I see secretaries in a much fuller role. They should be given the opportunity to utilize their skills.

Timing

Timing can be critical. Be at the wrong place at the wrong time and you're dead. Be at the right place at the right time and you're hired, promoted, transferred, married, or whatever.

I'm not a great believer in luck, but I have come to appreciate the importance of timing. Inventing a completely effective diphtheria vaccine today is of little value since diphtheria is of little threat anymore. However, inventing some means of deactivating nuclear radiation would make one an instant hero. You can't always control timing but you need to keep it in mind.

Vision

Vision is one quality that I have found to set managers apart. It is also a luxury. Most managers are required to keep the status quo but research managers are expected to make changes, and it is this license to make change that demands vision. What surprises me is that so few research managers appear to have vision. Upon reflecting on this, I realized that many research directors are really running technical service groups and are paid to make incremental improvements in a defined process, not to come up with radical solutions to national or global problems. Thus, vision isn't as critical. But if one manages scientists in an organization that deals with real, significant problems, vision is critical.

I don't think anyone has a crystal ball, but I do think a good manager has to keep an interest in a large number of fields so that she can have an awareness of overriding problems facing humankind, select those that are related to the organization's mission, and help cross-fertilize the scientists to help solve the problems.

In answering the question, "Why is vision so important?" Warren Bennis said, as quoted by Browne (1986), "Without it, there is no sense in communicating, there's no sense in persisting, and there's no sense in applying yourself.

All organizations that are in trouble either have no vision or they get mixed messages about what their vision is" (2).

REFERENCES

Section 1

1. S. P. Blake, "Managing For Responsive Research and Development," (San Francisco, CA: W.H. Freeman and Co., 1978), Chapter 5.

Section 2

1. U.S. Federal Council for Science and Technology, "The Environment for Quality," Report of the Standing Committee, Donald F. Hornig, chairman. Washington, D.C., December 1966, p. 4.

2. Industrial Research, "Researchers Prefer West--but Rank Job and Salary Higher," Industrial Research, May 1966, p. 97.

3. U.S. Department of Health, Education, and Welfare, "Improving the Environment for Science in DHEW," first report of the Career Service Board for Science, John C. Eberhart, chairman. Washington, D.C., December 1968, p. 12.

4. T. J. Allen, "Managing the Flow of Technology," (Cambridge, MA: The MIT Press, 1979), p. 232.

Section 3

1. J. R. Hinrichs, "High-Talent Personnel," AMA, 1986, p. 203.

2. J. Balderston, "Successful Administration of a Research Laboratory," Research/Development, June 1969, p. 24.

3. Ibid. p. 28.

4. Hinrichs, op. cit. p. 213.

5. P. F. Drucker, "Management," (New York: Harper and Row, 1974), p. 790.

6. A. H. Maslow, "A Theory of Human Motivation," Psychological Review, July 1943, p. 370.

7. T. R. Masterson and T. G. Mara, "Motivating the Underperformer," AMA, 1969, p. 10.

8. E. Raudsepp, "Managing Creative Scientists and Engineers," (New York: Macmillan Co., 1963), p. 170.

9. D. D. McConkey, "MBO for Non-Profit Organizations," AMA, 1975.

10. Drucker, op. cit. p. 797.

Section 4

1. F. J. Roethlisberger, "Man-in-Organization," (Cambridge, MA: Belknap Press of Harvard University, 1968), p. 154.

2. D. C. Pelz and F. M. Andrews, "Scientists in Organizations," (New York: John Wiley & Sons, Inc., 1966), p. 39.

3. M. R. Feinberg, "Effective Psychology for Managers," (Englewood Cliffs, NJ: Prentice-Hall, Inc., 1966).

4. E. Raudsepp, "Managing Creative Scientists and Engineers," (New York: Macmillan Co., 1963) p. 223.

5. U.S. Federal Council for Science and Technology, "The Environment for Quality," Report of the Standing Committee, Donald F. Hornig, chairman. Washington, D.C., December 1966, p. 4

6. U.S. Department of Health, Education, and Welfare, "Improving the Environment for Science in DHEW," First report of the Career Service Board for Science, John C. Eberhart, chairman. Washington, D.C., December 1968, p. 12.

7. Raudsepp, op. cit. p. 224.

8. G. Jewkes, P. Thompson, and G. Dalton, "Research Management," (January 1979), p. 15.

Section 5

1. P. F. Drucker, "Management," (New York: Harper & Row, 1974), p. 142.

2. E. R. Browne, "Leadership," (1986), p. 30.